Contents

THUNDER BOLTS

Wild Places

by
David Orme

Rans:m

Thunderbolts

Wild Places
by David Orme

Illustrated by Ellie Foreman-Peck

Published by Ransom Publishing Ltd.
Radley House, 8 St. Cross Road, Winchester, Hants. SO23 9HX, UK
www.ransom.co.uk

ISBN   978 178127 076 9

First published in 2013

Wild Places:
The Facts

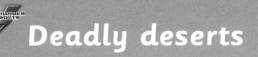

Deadly deserts

A desert is a place that doesn't get enough rain. It is a difficult place for wildlife and people to live.

Why do deserts happen?

Rain falling

No rain

Desert

Sometimes deserts are dry because there are mountains nearby. The rain falls on the mountains. There is no water left for the desert.

Sometimes deserts happen because the climate in the area changes and gets drier.

Sometimes people make deserts by not looking after the land properly.

Fact file: The Gobi desert

The Gobi desert is a tough place to live.

In summer the temperature can be 50 degrees.
In winter it can be minus 40 degrees.

Some animals and plants
still manage to live here.

Rock lizard

Gazelle

Amazing fact: The Gobi desert is one of the best places in the world to find dinosaur remains.

This shows it wasn't always a desert.

Fantastic rainforests

Deserts are a tough place for wildlife, but wildlife loves rainforests!

Just 2 square kilometres of rainforest may have:

- over 50,000 different sorts of insects
- nearly 500 different types of trees!

The rainforest's most amazing animals – ants!

- Ants keep herds of other insects, just like humans keep sheep or cows.

- They grow plant crops.

- They build shelters.

- If it floods, they can even build boats!

Fact file: Amazing Amazon

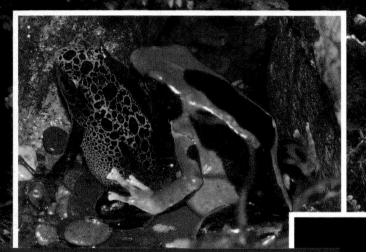

The Amazon rainforest is the biggest in the world. It covers half a million square kilometres.

One in ten of all the different living things in the world are found here:

- Two and half million different types of insect

- 40,000 different types of plants

- 800 different mammals

- 300 different reptiles

- Over 3,000 different birds

- 1,000 different frogs!

Mega mountains

Why are mountains cold?

When you go high, the air gets thinner.
Thin air can't hold so much heat.

Very high mountains may have glaciers.
These are like frozen rivers.

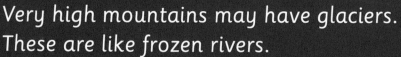

What lives on mountains?

The very tops of high mountains are a tough place to live. Nothing grows there, and it is hard to breathe because of the thin air.

Lower down there are plenty of animals and plants.

Mountain goat

The Himalayan mountains

The Himalayas are the highest mountains in the world. Over 100 mountains in the Himalayas are over 7,200 metres high.

Mount Everest is the highest, is that right?

Yes, that's right. It is 8,848 metres high.

Is it easy to climb?

No! It's very cold, and above 8,000 feet there isn't enough oxygen to breathe properly. This is called the DEATH ZONE.

Climbers usually take extra oxygen with them.

Lonely islands – Easter Island

Easter Island is in the Pacific Ocean. It is a very remote place.

In 1600 about 15,000 people lived there. By 1870 only about 100 were left.

Why?

- Climate change made life difficult.

- Visitors to the islands brought diseases.

- Some people were taken as slaves.

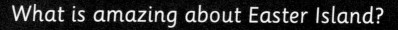

What is amazing about Easter Island?

These statues! Nearly 900 of them were made between 1100 and 1600.

Cold places – northern Canada

This part of Canada is huge – and very empty!

The land in the far north is known as tundra. There are no trees, and the ground is frozen.

A really important animal in the north of
Canada is the caribou. There are seven
times as many caribou as there are people!

In the past, the Inuit people of northern
Canada needed the caribou for food,
and to make clothes, shelter and tools.

Keeping them wild

The world is full of wonderful wild places. But there are problems.

The world's weather is changing. This can damage wild places.

Mining for metal happens in wild places.

There are more and more people in the world. People need food.

Forests are being cut down to make space to grow more food. Too many fish are being taken from the sea.

How can we save these wild places?

Save Our Wood!

Kim loved Oaktree Wood. She went there every week.

She kept a video diary of all the plants and animals she found there.

One day Kim had a shock. She saw a notice with really bad news!

One day ...

NO ENTRY
BUILDING SITE

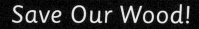

Kim met a man wearing a hard hat. He told her that the wood was going to be cut down.

The space was needed for a car park for a new factory.

Kim was really upset.

She decided to post her video diary on the Internet.

People loved Kim's videos.

Everyone was really cross when they found out what was going to happen to the wood. They told all their friends online.

Then something amazing happened!

Kim was asked to do an interview for TV.

She explained why the wood was so important.

She had started something big!

At last, the owner of the new factory came to the wood.

He had an announcement to make.

It was great news, especially for Kim!

Word list

Amazon	Inuit
breathe	kilometre
caribou	mammal
climate	mountain
desert	rainforest
Easter Island	reptile
explain	temperature
gazelle	tough
Gobi	tundra
goat	video
Himalayas	